Volcanoes Shaping Earth

Ariana Lucarelli

Rosen Readers

Rosen Classroom™

New York

Published in 2014 by The Rosen Publishing Group, Inc.
29 East 21st Street, New York, NY 10010

Book Design: Mickey Harmon

Photo Credits: Cover beboy/Shutterstock.com; p. 5 Pablo Hidalgo/Shutterstock.com; p. 13 Jason Patrick Ross/Shutterstock.com; p. 15 Jonathan Vasata/Shutterstock.com; p. 17 Tim Roberts Photography/Shutterstock.com; p. 19 Neonblak/Wikipedia.org; p. 21 SCIENCE PHOTO LIBRARY/Science Photo Library/Getty Images; p. 22 Lemonpink Images/Shutterstock.com.

ISBN: 978-1-4777-2412-5
6-pack ISBN: 978-1-4777-2414-9

Manufactured in the United States of America

CPSIA Compliance Information: Batch #CS13RC: For further information contact Rosen Publishing, New York, New York at 1-800-237-9932.

Contents

Earth Changes

Earth is always changing. The changes can be both slow and fast. Fast changes are usually caused by forces of nature that act on Earth's land. This includes volcanoes (vahl-KAY-nohz).

Volcanoes are openings in Earth's **crust** that allow melted rock, ash, and gases to come aboveground. They can teach us why Earth looks the way it does.

The word "volcano" comes from Vulcan, the name of the Roman god of fire.

What's Inside Earth?

Volcanoes may look like mountains, but there's more going on inside than meets the eye. Instead of being solid, volcanoes have hollow tubes called vents. The vents lead down into a pool of melted rock, called magma.

Magma collects in the magma chamber. The heat and **pressure** in the magma chamber force the magma up through the vent and out of the volcano's opening, called the crater.

Volcanoes are openings into Earth.
Can you name all the parts?

Inside a Volcano

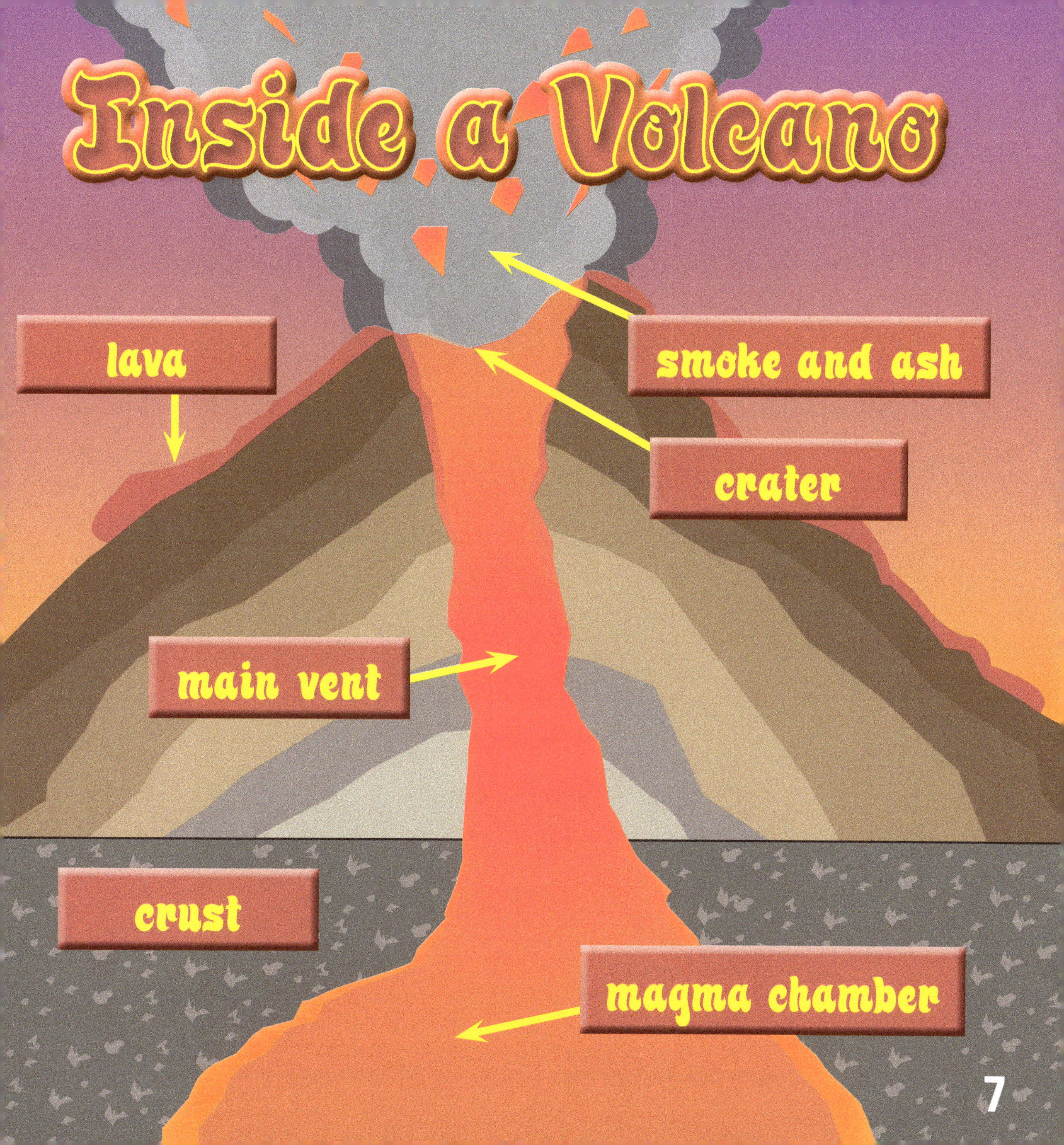

Earth's crust is made of plates. The plates fit together like pieces of a puzzle. They don't stay still, though. They're always moving, just very slowly. In some places, plates move apart. In other places, they rub against each other.

Magma may be created in places where plates meet. Can you guess what this makes? If you said volcanoes, you're right!

We can tell where Earth's plates come together simply by looking at where volcanoes are.

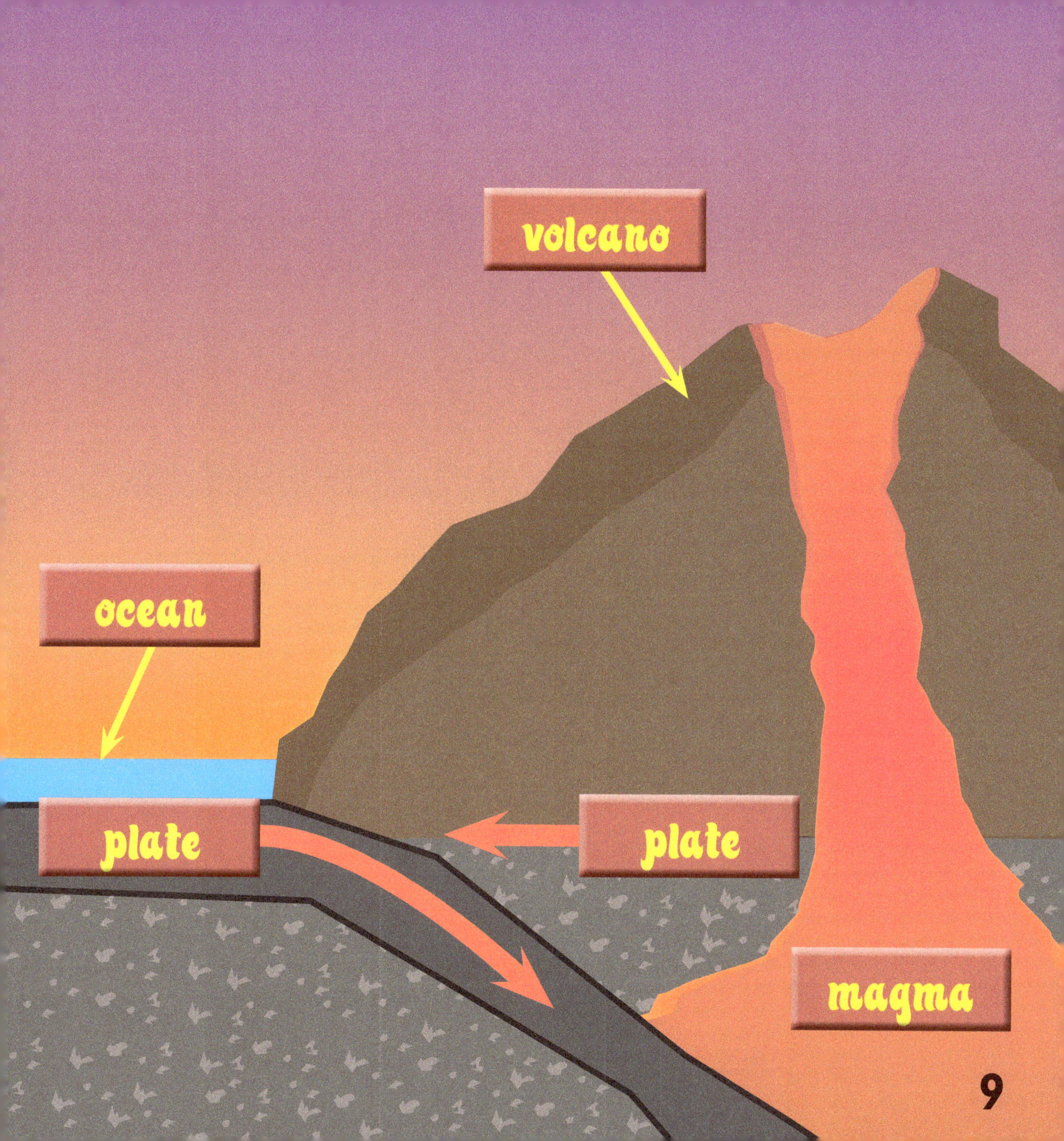
volcano
ocean
plate
plate
magma

Lava

When magma comes aboveground, it's called lava. The lava is really hot. It cools and hardens as time passes. Once it cools, it turns into solid rock.

Most of the cracks in Earth's crust are in the ocean floors. Lava has always flowed from these cracks. Over millions of years, the newer rock built up on top of the older rock. This created mountains and islands.

Most of the world's volcanoes are in the Ring of Fire. It's an area around the Pacific Ocean where some of Earth's plates meet.

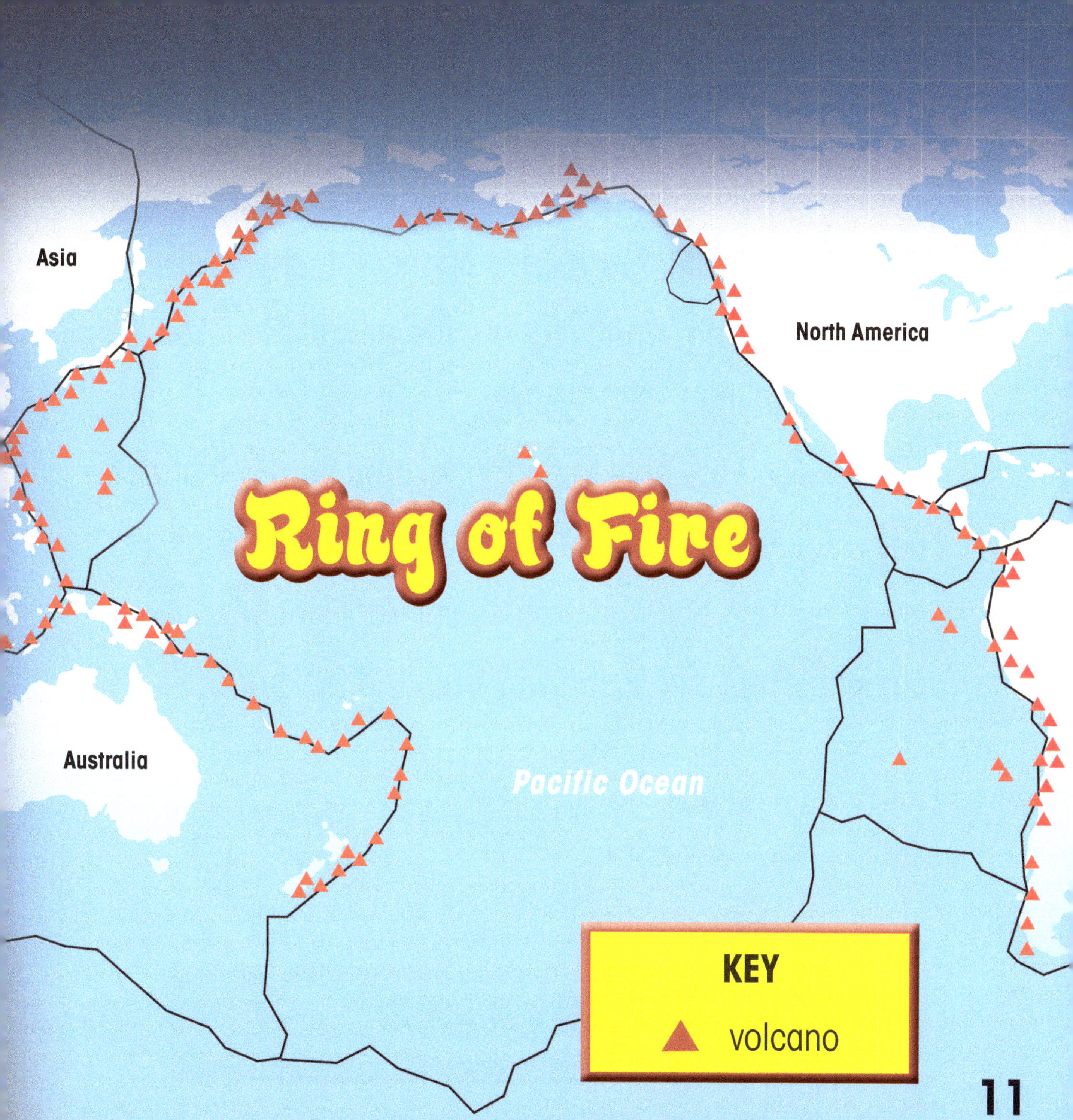
Ring of Fire
Asia
North America
Australia
Pacific Ocean
KEY
volcano

The way lava flows causes changes to the land around a volcano. When it cools, the new rock makes the land look different.

Lava isn't the only thing that **erupts** from volcanoes. They also give off ash and gas. The way these things spread out and build up creates different kinds of volcanoes. This affects the way our land looks, too.

This rock was created when lava cooled. It wasn't there before the volcano erupted!

Types of Volcanoes

The first kind of volcano is a stratovolcano (strah-toh-vohl-KAY-noh). It looks like a very tall mountain. Stratovolcanoes have steep sides and a small crater. This makes it hard for magma to escape easily. When it does escape, it causes a very powerful eruption.

Stratovolcanoes release a lot of lava, gas, and ash. They build up in **layers**, which makes the volcano taller and steeper.

There are 452 stratovolcanoes in the Ring of Fire. The Ring of Fire looks like a big mountain range, but it's really a lot of volcanoes.

Cinder cone volcanoes are the simplest type of volcano. When they erupt, the lava breaks into small pieces as it blasts into the air. The small pieces settle and harden in a wide circle around the volcano's opening. This creates a bowl-shaped crater.

Unlike stratovolcanoes, cinder cone volcanoes aren't very tall. They're also found in a different part of the world.

Many cinder cone volcanoes are found in North America.

Another type of volcano is a shield volcano. It's a wide volcano with gently rising sides. These volcanoes are formed from lava that flows easily. It doesn't erupt into the air. It just spills over the sides and spreads out.

Most volcanoes on Earth are shield volcanoes. The Hawaiian Islands were built from them. Hawaii looks different from most places on Earth thanks to its volcanoes!

Can you see this volcano is wider and flatter than the others?

Active, Extinct, or Dormant?

Active volcanoes erupt often, so they're always shaping Earth. Extinct volcanoes are ones that will never erupt again. They were active a long time ago.

Dormant volcanoes haven't erupted for a long time, but could in the future. There's a lot of magma built up in them, so when they do erupt, it's powerful! Dormant volcanoes have caused some of the world's worst volcanic eruptions.

Mount St. Helens was a dormant stratovolcano until it erupted on May 18, 1980.
It was the worst eruption in U.S. history.

Plants Around Volcanoes

Volcanic ash and gases affect our land, too. They break down into the ground around the volcano. This puts **minerals** into the soil. The minerals make the soil rich, which makes plants healthy.

Volcanoes are some of the coolest things on Earth! Learning about them helps us understand why our world looks the way it does.

Glossary

crust (KRUHST) The top layer of Earth's land.

erupt (ih-RUHPT) To give off lava, ash, and gas.

layer (LAY-uhr) One thickness of something over or under another.

mineral (MIH-nuh-ruhl) A nonliving matter that's part of Earth.

pressure (PREH-shur) The act of pressing.

Index